ALMOST DARK

Almost Dark

Poems by

Richard Terrill

For John,
Fellow poet
and friend
Dick Terrill

University of Tampa Press

Cover photo by Jurek Durczak

Manufactured in the United States of America
Printed on acid-free paper ∞
First Edition

The University of Tampa Press
401 West Kennedy Boulevard
Tampa, FL 33606

ISBN 978-1-59732-076-4 (hbk.)
ISBN 978-1-59732-077-1 (pbk.)

Browse & order online at
http://utpress.ut.edu

Library of Congress Cataloging-in-Publication Data

Terrill, Richard, 1953-
Almost dark : poems / by Richard Terrill. – 1st ed.
p. cm.
ISBN 978-1-59732-076-4 (cloth : acid-free paper)
ISBN 978-1-59732-077-1 (pbk. : acid-free paper)
I. Title.
PS3620.E767A79 2010
811'.6–dc22 2010004865

Contents

We are here on Earth to fart around,
and don't let anybody tell you different.

–Kurt Vonnegut

From the heart, may it go to the heart.

–Ludwig van Beethoven
(*Missa Solemnis*)

For Tse Fung-Kuen

Ideas of Order

Use this book
as the fourth leg of a three-legged table.
Use this book as a dart,
or a rhythm that repeats over many measures,
the bending of palms in storm.

Use these words as temporary disease, permanent cure.
As sine wave, ocean wave, or wave goodbye
from the deck of a ship,
the month-long crossing.
Who needs this book?
The poor, who pick up our bones?

How this book is organized:
not very well, and a little less each page.
It's easy to be organized
if all you want

is to be organized. The moon skips a month
and appears twice in one sky,
and how foolish you feel
as victim of its blue trick,
double shadows of the roadster on an evening drive.
Try to make meaning, not a living
from this book.

Consider these sentences a restatement of streetlight
on the summer street.
Consider what happens if meditation finally works. Then what?
Your weak mind won't simply hand you
a sky full of limes, a garden stocked
with words or dirigibles, a doomed crab.

Last year something happened to make the juncos rest.
The spirea stopped growing in the yard.

The grown children moved home,
their eyes devoid of stars,
no entrée to the upper middle class,
no training as shaman or broker,
their memories toxic with summer.

What to look for in a poem:
a warning. Make a list
of all the ins and outs, the sins and wars.
List all the examples
that seek conclusions to support.

We sometimes feel, don't we, a little
like statistics before the crime,
guilty for not having cleaned up well, having wished
our lives away, wishing the sun
would go down at last.
Well, it did.

I

Deer, December

One of thirty nights I can't sleep
I awaken to motion in the last dark
out the window, tight against the hillside.
I put on my glasses to stop
the glass in the old house from wavering.

Three of them, maybe twenty feet away,
they nuzzle new snow,
leaves and twigs not yet frozen hard,
a poor diet, winter just begun.
Foraging, chewing, staring lines into space.
Their necks bolt upright only to the slight
shift in what I imagine is wind,
to things I can't hear, couldn't,
were I with them outside and not still
warm on the edge of the bed.

Then a cardinal is winter
red against the even gray of 6 a.m.
—cloudy, this time of year. I'll stay watching
until I'm late for another morning meeting,
my alarm clock not gone off—that must be it.
I can't know how little I'll be missed.

The Past

1.

It tells you everything
you believe is true,
is true for everyone.

It holds up half the sky.

It is black and white and dead all over.
It wears the same tattered plaid
sport coat every time you notice,
the one your father wore,
old pipe tobacco loose in the pockets.

It is an anchor, it weighs nothing.
It is a doorstop, it props open
the door to that place
—the many pictures, the constant themes

whose thoughts won't walk away,
whose waist is a call for murder,
whose mouth calls to the sea.
whose tongue is not related,
whose tongue is a wafer
whose teeth get what they want.

2.

The shoulders of the past bring rain always, always
bring rain whose wrists, fingers, hands
are indistinguishable from filament, pavement, establishment,
a mint dissolving on the tongue.

The insides of watches, the workings of the nervous system
have nothing on the past. It exists

beyond comment or controversy,
light in a telescope's mirror. The past

whose secret is longing, whose longing is secret,
whose secrets are a carriage over potted roads,
whose longing is something to look backward to.

Why does it rain so much in the past
and no one ever gets wet?
The principals in this drama have died.
Why do the prevailing winds blow no sand from this beach?

The Father's Room

1.

The nursing home aide, the good one, ex-nun
with the patience of a distant planet,
sets down the phone, goes
to check the father's room.

The silence too long, the connection so perfect
that the son hears her footsteps come back
to say he's just that minute gone,
"*Just as you were dialing . . .* "

Why does the son assume
he is the only one crying
as if in an empty theater,
darkness rising toward the chandeliers?

Friends can't take him past the irony last moments make,
the *He just had said*, the *Only last week*,
the *He finished all his supper that night*
and asked for coffee and dessert.

The idea comes then, and passes, that death gives meaning.
The dying, at first, seems to reveal something.

2.

We hauled him up to the cabin one time last year.
More at ease, he didn't insist on packing a rifle
—what did he think we were going to shoot?—didn't insist
on taking his car, not driven since winter.

He even showed mild interest in the two plum trees
I'd planted in the yard, warned me again
to keep the beaver from rebuilding in the lagoon

where only last May he waded with hip boots to tear up their lodge,

got stuck in mud so deep my mother called the rescue squad.
He warned me not to leave valuables inside when I closed up,
so far back in the woods they'd just as soon steal as look at you.
He told me this season we'd hunt from the deer stand the bears clawed to hell.

He told me this property was no good for deer,
and why that was so.

The Lighthouse

My mother holds my hand,
my wife on her other side,
and lightly toes the beach.

She walks over "tricky rocks,"
steps over puddles from a week of rain.
We pass the spring-sweet smell of birch.

Fifteen minutes—do you
want to turn around now? Twenty?
She's 89 and has lost count.

She wishes she could see her house,
sold last week, one more time; her lack
of complaint complements the evening.

Do you want to walk all the way to the lighthouse?

Now the waves thin to gloss on stones.
The moon is up, the sun not down
over the Great Lake, catching

the tops of white pine on the island,
then the top of the lighthouse on shore,
then nothing.

"If you take bigger steps,
you don't have to take as many," she says.
The paper says the neighbors want

that old lighthouse torn down:
it attracts too many tourists,
people taking walks on their shore.

"Why do they want to tear down
that nice light house?"
Mother asks. Then an orange nodding

flower in the grass. "Buttercup?"
She used to know wildflowers,
but she forgot, bends down

too quickly, remembers, picks
a white dandelion,
and blows the seeds away.

"Spring Can Really Hang You Up the Most"

The smell of something burning is last summer's cutworm moth
dried in the frosted bowl of the floor lamp on the screened porch.
I rush the season and read out there,
dark just after six, chilly well before five.

The neighbor kids' swing set still packed away,
their dad plays country radio,
combs the soggy lawn with a garden rake,
pulling white grass out by its roots like old hair.

I can't tell in the dark if the lake ice is too thin to dance on,
if the groceries in their weariness have frozen
these still-short afternoons, forgotten in the car.
Snowmelt gathers on tennis courts in the park.

Evenings, I try drinking more,
less, not at all. Beer, gin, Sumatran blend.
The fresh tea a former student sent us from Fujian
packs a better jolt, but the second cup wears off too soon.

I alphabetize my poetry collections,
straighten out the kitchen drawer with the little spice jars in it.
Each morning I check the daffodils' lack-of-progress in the perennial bed
that by mid-summer my wife will call "the valley of death."

It's almost spring the way it's almost morning
when somebody wakes you in the middle of the night.
I want to wake Linda from the silence she's calling sleep,
wake her with a last meal, a lost romance, or the memory of it.

I want to bother her with some pretty good cheap wine,
bother her with that iris of night around an April moon,
(bother her like the bird
about to use her eyelash in its nest).

We're weightlessness, half awake,
trampoline before the rain comes back.
I can't tell if rhyme is slowing down the growing cloud mass.
I can't tell if we should have paid someone to sing.

I Kept the Part about Turning Fifty

More on the theme of suddenly finding yourself at middle age
and less perhaps about memories that are more telling to the writer than the reader.
–Rejection Slip

So I lost the part about walking to school,
the new subdivision after the war, unfinished,
cutting through Kocha's field with all the dandelions
(or a calf-high puddle of slush we waded in March),
passing Ma Whiting's house, the beer bottles, cigarette cartons
piled even above the trash can rim, still life-ing into the street,
the dead end where she lived with her seven kids and no husband,
how they ate jelly sandwiches. It was all they could afford,
our parents said. The piss and stale dirt smell
of her kids on the playground. One seemed to be named "Poopy."
You could hear everyone, even his mother, call that out after school
from the holey screen door, cigarette wrangling,
misshapen house dress, the house
with gray-green asphalt siding, the house
that must have been there when Kocha's was still a farm
and our yards planted in corn or beans.
"Poopy," she called, "Poopy, get in here."
Her voice gruff as old stone
smashed along their unpaved driveway.

I decided to cut the scene
where Miss Campbell, first grade, huffs
and pulls a Whiting girl by her stained smock
to the sink like the one in back of every room.
She bends the girl under the faucet,
lathers a hand soap to froth
and washes the dirty girl's hair,
fingers ram straight, but hands moving gently, effective
through the tangle that surely becomes dark blond.
The suds cascade to the beige countertop,

down the face of the pine cabinet
where the art supplies were kept and, I remember,
onto the checkerboard tile of the cold floor.

November 22

You remember where but not who you were
—ten years old and waiting on the steps
outside Norwood school just after lunch,
the old part of the building, which dated from the teens,
and a girl named Jane Process running up saying,
"I hope he dies!" And you, playground-wise,

knowing a story when you heard one. Then
Miss Parliek—an old woman (all were)
who looked, you thought, like a large thumb,
frumpy and well-intentioned, your fifth grade teacher,
coming out to tell the children it was so.

They let you in, all of you, and through
what should have been math, the scratchy intercom's
radio accounts, events unfolding
like books you hadn't read. You remember
sitting at your desk (but not just how
—hands folded, fidgeting with a ruler,
kicking mud flecks fallen from your shoes?).

And when they let out school, Miss Parliek looking through
the window at the flag, which happened
to be waving. Her short neck, slouching out.
The old part of the building, a dark day. About to rain some more.

How to Live

When I am alone, I am not happy.
The evening begins by afternoon,
the sky a thick unwhite.
It's flecked with doubt, doesn't talk,
but sits about the couch with a bag of snacks
and a silence almost evangelical
in its failure to discriminate.
The brown branches of the park hold great meaning.
The Christmas lights on the window of the little shop behind my flat:
A pattern? A secret handshake?
Whenever I reach my building entrance, jangle through keys,
I am greeted by the clacks of my double locks
something like those on my heart,
chain and dead bolt like gaudy jewelry.
Once inside, I am a grown child, strange to myself,
and memory a broken scale with its weighty notes.
Boredom dances with virtue,
all heels and tails, all steps rehearsed.
What did I plan to say to myself
when I got to the bottom of the day?

Eastern Poland, 2003

The old coffee haunts—drafty, unswept and ill lit—
have gone upscale: restaurants for the newly prosperous.
Nobody here has the post-Communist time
to just sit around and dream all day
of a different system, a better world
over a cup of spare coffee or watery

socialist tea. There's just this one shop left in town
—the fresh wallpaper scarlet, the new chairs
plush maroon, the drapes as posh and heavy
as those at Ford's Theater, the musak
in its desire to please as endearing as a small dog,
someone singing "Just the Way You Look Tonight."

The Poles may not know the practice
of jotting things down in coffee houses
run by lesbians or English major drop outs,
places with left wing newspapers in the racks
and bus-your-own bins of other people's latte,
mostly-eaten veggie wraps. There's

not a magazine rack in sight.
I'm trying to write,
am underdressed for the crowd. The beautiful
patrons sip and talk in twos and threes.
Greeting, they ghost kiss each cheek.
Parting, they rise all at once, like a jury.

What to Want

Here in Poland, dogs walk unleashed; their masters wander
a half block ahead or behind, no whistle or secret call.
The dogs sit patiently outside shops, over by a city tree struggling to grow;
sometimes in among the vegetables, or panting beneath the CD rack.

When the Nazis came in '39, it was not yet fall,
and after the Polonaise was broadcast one last time from the capital
no one considered doing what they were told;
that winter would be a little less, is all.

It's still a place full
of impenetrable waiting, the *now* sharp as snow
—which is cold when it falls,
warms when it hits the ground.

How do they train these dogs? My boyish neighbor girl,
the height of a teen but the hurry and gait of an American ten-year-old:
she greets me, *dzien dobry*, politely,
as she takes her terrier out to the park. I merely watch,

more captivated than by an afternoon at the Palace Museum
or in the streetmarket in front of Castle Square,
where the couples neck Sunday afternoons,
where the Jews were housed before the camps.

During the Communists, it was good form to fail Russian in school,
to read Western novels and listen to rock
in this country that has disappeared more times than a magician's assistant.
In '44, the resistance rose and the Russians merely camped

across the river, watched the retreating Germans quell
the partisans and burn Warsaw a flat grey.
The rebellion didn't subside; it's just that most of the rebels
were dead. Civilians shocked and drained the lakes

for something to eat. The dogs heel,
the action of doing what's best for oneself,
much like cueing for the tram,
happy the stores are stocked,

and one can finally stop waiting
for the Americans to come to the rescue.

The Little Dog

My dog is a bichon frise. It's a breed of Mediterranean French origin, but this dog, trained and passed on to us by my wife's family, understands only Cantonese. In order to be obeyed, I've built a vocabulary around bodily functions and expressions of pleasure and disapproval. *Gai gai* is "go for a walk," or literally, "outside outside." If, when we're alone and I can be myself, I tell him "you're a cute little *guy*," my dog hears only that last syllable and dances toward the door with a look of entitlement. He's not bilingual.

Awe sieh? means "do you need to poop?" *Qwai zhai* means "good boy." *Down* and *hey* seem part of a universal dialect—contradiction, disempowerment, not giving in to impulse and desire—that he sometimes pretends not to understand.

Chaw dai, and the dog sits at my feet.
M hou la, and he stops licking them.

The dog forgives my American accent. In fact, he's remarkable in many ways: barks at strangers, sleeps in the sun, feigns fear when I chase him around the house with my soprano saxophone playing "Calling All Pets."

Sik fan means eat rice (or dry dog food, in his case).
Deng deng means wait a little, as when, mornings,

the dog waits patiently at our closed bedroom door after he hears us stir. Or evenings, when he waits to be invited into my lap for screenings of rented art films—Goddard or Wong Kar Wai, he never complains. I sip my brandy; he rests his head on my thigh.

For the Chinese Elm and Flowering Crab

I'm like a guest in this house, my house.
Already I'm thinking of resale: prune
to keep the shrubs from bushing out,
clear the gutters too often of fallen branches.

In this, another suburb, "nature"
is merely what the trees stand for.
Non-native, ornamental, put-off-for-now.
The grass grows patchy under their branches.

In "Wild Geese on the Lake," Shen Yueh
has those birds come back each spring
to pre-Tang China, a few circling,
but all eventually giving in

to their winged consensus. In our Minnesota
cities and towns, pre-apocalypse,
the geese don't even leave in fall,
lazy on park walks, off-season golf courses,

in wetland set-asides described by expressways
or fenced off next to the parking lot
of the consignment store. It could be for beauty
we design such policy, don't shoot

the nuisance geese, the mess they make.
It could be we're desperate and do as much
as we can, as little as that is. The geese
are still here, staying on through

the succession of dynasties, and through our turn
around the block that makes a year.

The Old Neighborhood

None of these boys is supposed to play near the
Zoll Stone Company, Makers of Decorative Concrete Products.

Once there, they can sneak under the wire fence to watch the
waste drain gray green from the plant into the creek,
stuff hardened like magma along the bank
so they can pick up a chunk and chuck it at a friend and laugh.

Nearer home, one boy, maybe seven or eight, lies in the street,
teased to tears by the older brothers on the block.
They're not sure what to make of him, the older boys,
his arms Christlike, his wail a measure of their power.

He waits for a speeding car, or for someone
to tell him to get up, and why.

Grown and looking back, these boys might think
that the concept of soul is nostalgic, the soul antique,
which means it's worth whatever someone will pay for it.
They might think the soul can be lost in the waste

at the Zoll Stone Company, or lost in the street waiting
for a speeding car, or just lost in the housing of the body
—a three-bedroom rambler so small
that some people would do anything to move out.

Nostalgia says the moon used to rise higher. The sky
was darker at night, bluer during the day.
The poor side of town was still ok.

But now, even for a good price, the soul is hard to find.
It loiters sometimes at the corner of Fate and Madison, Hollywood and Time.
Torment on cold mornings in bed, sadness on too hot summer afternoons.
What happened today, what happened yesterday

—it's all just longing, I guess, as it intersects with loathing.
Everything is becoming too much,

even in the old neighborhood, where sun spoils
the baked ball diamond, the shuttered warehouse.
Power lines sag near the aging apartments, never gone condo,
their residents unmarried, widowed, almost dead,

or simply closer to the liquor store
and waiting for the money to run out.

Last Places
(north)

Maybe evening primrose against a threat of rain.
The silhouette of jack pine against the newsprint-surface
of a lake in wind.

Maybe drumming grouse in spring, the last spring,
a raven or gull undistinguished, indiscreet.
Sounds of wing beats.

The last place you can go
where no one has ever been
—maybe you won't even know you're there,

a place like a pocket of air.
A place curved
or written only in water,

a dry moment unremarkable
except for its existence
in a wet season.

Because some of the places weren't beautiful
they went unvisited right up to the moment
of their destruction,

gone the whir of the June bug,
the smallest scrap of birch paper.
Broken branches a network of contradictions.

When the places disappear
there will be only nowhere to go.
Even people not yet born will have changed

like an image to be painted on glass
and held to light,
the confusion of water for sky that a reflection makes.

Maybe rose hips in snow.
Angel configured in the stripped bark of a Norway pine.
Skeleton of cedar. The sleepless path to the lake.

Death will be meaningless without
the widowed places. No last encounters
with frozen shorelines or unfished streams.

No chance to accept
our undoing for the sake of what remains,
a red leaf in a dark pond.

Maybe a heron lifts away like a match set to tinder.
Or aurora borealis, the rising green and white light
on the day your father dies.

One letter in a white word, the last word.

II

Where It Stays

The first snow
the patches where it stays
on bare ground not grass
on the mud of construction sites
shards of black tarp
and worn metal in piles
or on the black valleys of a passing umbrella
as I see it and its person from my window above
(the paint has chipped from the sill)
and always
in the heart
that forbidden word
that second immediate world.

Since I was a boy there has been this falling
never direct
sometimes not to the ground
why do I watch
why do cars still pass not seeing
(me, or maybe even the snow)
why do the same buildings as always appear
through the white pores of morning
why do I question the draft from my window
on such a cold day?

A young master walks his shepherd
on the diagonal through the park
I can't help but look at from here
a crow changes to a better branch
willows keep their leaves in a strong wind
it's Poland
Sunday
people walk
I imagine

toward mass
I can't see their faces
weather aches in my back too long in bed
snow falls too at the end of longing.

Maybe there is a formula for its random swirl
the temperature at which blood freezes
the date at which the heart contracts
the angle of the missing sun the heart would rectify
the missing heart in the moving present
the snowy arrangement of buildings/cars/walkers
and shadows in the heart's best view
how shadow exists even in the deepest November gray
the small rage of old leaves covered on the ground now
the mottled reflections puddles make on an uneven street.

I can hear ostinato in the silence
hear mass on TV from the next apartment
the young woman who lives there
last night at ten
sang arias for her applauding guests
her voice is thin
but her pitch at least is good.

O dwóch takich, co ukradli księżyc

Oh they were lazy,
The Two Boys Who Stole the Moon,

the terrible twins, Jacek and Placek.
When they were babies
their mother would chew the dry crusts
and kiss the mash into their mouths like nestlings.

They stole because they were poor. Their father gone
to another town, their mother raised them alone.
They stole the moon and ran away.
Or did they run away and then

steal the moon, desperate at the end?
They thought the moon slept in the swamp,
so they picked it and put it in their sack.
Of course they really had nothing. Who had anything

in those days? They argued over which
of them would carry the rich weight,
a loaf of bread or a wedge of cheese
drying yellow to gold.

Our grandparents knew
the movie version of this story
as intimately as Stalin's pock marks.
The actor who was Placek is now the mayor of Warsaw;

Jacek, a reformed thief, now minister of justice,
and leader of the opposition party.
Who is surprised by anything nowadays?
Everything in Poland is absurd

and simply so. After martial law,
the boys who stole the moon

became a cartoon,
which is why we know it, those of us

who were children then and don't remember Stalin's imperfections.
We grew up together like stalks of corn
in rows that sometimes got rain and elsewhere
remained dry as crust. Everything

is animation now, a children's story
that never really happened.

American

He would give you the shirt off his back
if he thought you wouldn't get it dirty.
He'd give you the dirt from his grave

if he thought he was ever going to die
and knew you wouldn't be there with a wad of spit
collecting in your dark cheek,

knew you wouldn't be there holding a pistol
in the dark streets of his smoking city,
wired to a bomb in the bright districts

of his rubble on TV.
He drinks a quart of milk a day,
never been sick in his life!

Canadians flock to his doctors;
up there birds die in the streets.
He has worked so hard to get

what is his that others want. Opportunity
is a door neither open nor closed,
but silver or gold, and in reach.

In his church, no one asks
God's blessing
but exclaims that it is theirs.

In his story one moon rises, sure and shining,
He thinks he's at a dinner party,
and everyone else is too in awe to leave.

Marriage Encounter

Yesterday Earl told how after his second suicide attempt
he'd found his third wife Jackie,
and though his sex drive was not
what it was, you never know.
Viane confessed the details of her affair
and how Dwaine had forgiven her, though not his best friend.
At our wedding,

we had two witnesses, our former minister,
and a friend to take pictures (the camera didn't work),
the best man's wife there, too,
because it was her living room
and she hadn't left for work yet,
hadn't left the best man yet for the other guy.
We all went to lunch.

Today, Eve, a shaman and breast cancer survivor,
abused by her father,
who has found Judy, the love of her life,
bids us come forth two by two
to the gas fireplace in the Great Room of the Lodge,
and share with the group the commitment vows
we were supposed to have written last night.

"About those times I walked out or you did, or hung up,
broke a glass or smashed an old pot on the countertop
over I can't remember what? We do that less now.
'Romance?' you often tell friends,
'We skipped that part . . .' "

Facilitators pair our lounge chairs face to face,
side by side, light more candles and suggest,
to the wail of Celine Dion,
that we whisper forgiveness to each other.

And if there is nothing big to forgive,
just say something smaller and wait.

23 Short Poems about Love

a series of moments like blackbirds
that flock and turn
over the field

*

do we travel for this? dislocation of the heart,
well worn? what's that tree
out the window, flowering so late in fall?

*

the poplars stand all the same height
in their one straight row

*

when one train passes another,
that shush of speed and sound,
its blur in the window
the repetition of figures like yourself

*

no matter how old, how much
we scare into flight
the birds we most resemble

*

the smaller the paper the larger the word,
the grayer the sky the more anticipated light

*

or when a third gets off an elevator,
the two remaining shift
to put the greatest distance between

*

circumstance a pin around which
all roads must turn

*

a pint of circumstance
a quart of night
a tablespoon of foolishness
two tablespoons

*

bags and packs unpacked,
zen stones on the floor

*

beginning a sentence
when you already know how it ends
and make no judgment

*

I put on mozart's *requiem* glad
I'm not dead myself

*

the moon of pleasure and pain
held with one face to our face

*

to begin, we must first see
each other on that rock, among those trees,
each looking

*

a private correspondence between two parts of the same
obsession, blinds closed against light
and the shadows it would cast

*

tv news report: we just don't know
who killed the children and why

*

the young man writes
if I could be two places at once
I'd be with you both times

but the longing for another life is deep

*

a puppy so young
it doesn't know it exists
off the leash

*

look at your watch
its usher glow
in the theater dark
neither now nor goodbye

fate is merely retrospection, isn't it?

*

the days are getting longer
for a few more nights

Lines Abandoned by My Students

In their poems two things always happen at once:
a sigh as two memories intertwine,
or breath on cold window glass
while lovers lie on wrinkled sheets.
Cigarettes are never lit by the person smoking them,
the moon never not apparent through the trees.

It was the year of four family funerals,
The year the rain fell red and we tired of grief.
All fall the deer stole apples from our backyard;
All winter our skin dried to crust.

I find a sheaf of their lines in an envelope,
a forgotten exercise they scribbled in class
—the tall bleached blonde, for instance, svelte and tight
as rope, who on Day One announced her dream:
to be the next Katie Couric.
Or the guy who liked to make up stories

that sounded like movies from some old war.
And the woman about to graduate:
smartest in the class, she seldom spoke.
Her poems rearranged muscle and bone,
left starbursts on wrists and the small of backs.
Late semester, she moved in with her boyfriend in Duluth.

It was the year of shallow rivers, of butterflies
In the grass, plush and green,
The crunch of cinders in our driveway.
The silos swayed, capped by light. It was the time

Of cotton stirred up from dandelions
Like people in a field,
Only quieter, much quieter.
It was the year the daffodils wept.

Religion

And speaking of food, I'm reading in a book on Vermeer
that seventeenth century artists in the low countries liked
to portray religious subjects in the kitchen.
I doubt that's the reason my father and uncles
gathered there at family cocktail parties.
It's not that they weren't churchgoers,

just no need to talk that way. No
saints or martyrs at the cookfire, no redeemer
with the bread and simple milkmaids, but fluorescent light
falling evenly on their highball glasses (which never
clinked as that cliché goes, but *rattled*
—more booze, little mix, and lots of ice).

Their unfiltered cigarettes burned to apt conclusions,
waving in their hands to make a point:
Eisenhower duped again by the Ruskies,
Lombardi too East Coast to stay in Green Bay,
rock and roll music all just noise.
Any topic in this kitchen *but* religion. The appliances

all agleam in white, the food cleared away,
the women roosted smokeless in the living room
with Bailey's or Bristol Cream after the meal.
Was the living room meant for living? Maybe they thought so.
The dishes were done. And speaking of dishes, I don't
have one now, eating, bent over a book

of Vermeer prints overdue at the college library.
Crumbs from a roll and droplets of tea spill
from my cup, from my lip, fall to the red rump
of Saint Praxedis, an early work, whose subject
squeezes the blood of a decapitated martyr from a sponge
(though not a kitchen sponge . . .) into a ewer.

One uncle could remember when his mother
would chop the head off a chicken
right in the backyard, the old house,
Sundays, the train going by. That one bird
would have to be supper for the family of twelve.
I wipe my tea away with a sweatshirt sleeve,

relieved not to stain the book that isn't mine.
The uncles likely never saw a Vermeer,
nor knew him from any Belgian in town.

Credit

I couldn't do the assignment for today because I know in my heart that God wouldn't want me to read something like that.

When a writer writes "fuck," or a boy soldier in a story dreams of pussy,
some virgin by the lake back home, or a woman gets raped
against the side of an old Dodge, the fenders and torn clothing
seething against imagination, I assure you
that reading about it won't improve your life.

The Dao says your life has a limit but knowledge has none,
which sounds like something I would say in class,
until you read the part where the Dao says
striving for knowledge is pointless.
Maybe it's a bad translation.

I'm disturbed by the strip mall they're erecting south of campus,
where I used to bike to hear the first peepers in a marsh,
in mid-April—that time when dirty snow
might still mound in the aprons of driveways
and beneath evergreen boughs.

I can't stop progress, so I won't shop there—that strip mall—
or take my taxes to be done, buy a six-pack, haircut, burger, decaf.
God wouldn't want me to. I know that in my gut,
a feeling I get when I can't sleep. I never buy much anyway, just want,
in my emptiness, to be. When Neuh Chi

four times asked a question of Wang Ni, and four times
Wang Ni said he didn't know the answer, Neuh Chi understood
and danced with glee and told the Master, who replied,
"Are you just finding *that* out *now*?" Today, the wetland drained,
I biked near the overpass at the edge of town.

There's no trail so I took to the shoulder
when trucks went by, trespassed abandoned farm sites

and mown lawns of rich guys' estates to the river.
I found my own way, as you must.
So will I give you credit for the assignment? Excellent question.

Un Chien Andalou

there's so much to say at any one
time and still people talk too much, especially writers,
who also write too much.

what about the thing
gone unsaid, and why they can't leave it
alone?

how about a little sympathy for the inarticulate?
if you want inarticulateness
I'm your man.

here's to the ill-formed phrase, limping or fallen and
unable to get
up.

here's to the object not shackled to metaphor
the way the frothing lover in the Buñuel film
is shackled

to two dead steers he drags
toward a naked mademoiselle.
here's to the moon

that's just a moon bisected by a cloud, not a tenor
for the vehicle of eyeball
Dali slit

with a razor blade in that film's first scene,
the one that shows up in all the
textbooks, and that blob

of goo slurping out
from that eye
—they actually

used a dead sheep's eye for that.
you can read about it in any book.
so here's to that, to finding out

what you shouldn't believe
—what you see in some movie,
what you hear.

What to Write

Whenever I tried to write, my father said,
"Rick is doing his typing." He didn't know,
and suggested after college a job as a stenographer
or maybe the post office, with that good union,
the days before going postal meant
enacting your own final solution.
What to want? A painless death?

Location location location?
A bowl of borscht and plate of *pierogi ruskie*
at the "Communist" restaurant my Polish boss hates
because it reminds him of the days before "the changes"?
The meatless Ruskie dumpling is not really Russian,
but Poles always thought their crass neighbors too poor
for anything but the potatoes and cheese inside.

Are you sobbing nights? I'm not. Though the blonde
furniture in my flat, the slender girl a floor above,
her beloved untrained terrier, his sore neck and wandering impulse;
the grand and pleasant way the tourist hotels are lit next
to the main post office in my home city
where I don't speak the language and thus don't speak—all of this
leaves me inconsolable, ignored.

But I'm not crying, I'm typing. Still.
We must play the instruments they hand out in therapy
convincingly enough to merit discharge,
that long way home. Downtown,
pieces of broken English
people the walls with their disrespect:
"Motor to my hooligan," "fuct the world."

Found Poems

I make starting lineups from my older cousin's football and baseball cards
—unstack them, unstick them, breaking brittle rubber bands.
I fan them on the table, study the winning combinations:
Jackie Robinson, Doak Walker, Sid Luckman, Pee Wee Reese.
The DiMaggios, Dom and Joe. The poses are obvious as merlot:
gritting linemen, vaulting backs. One shortstop stretches like an old boot.

Some years' shots are black and white, and one series has dyed the athletes
in bright primary colors, no shades or tints, only faces in natural gray.
All the cards are worth good cash, but I don't care.
I copy down the language on the back:

Sid Hudson—pitcher: "*At one time most feared.*
Had blazing fastball—good curve. But arm suddenly went dead in '47."
What happened that season? Or in '48?
It doesn't say, and that's what's good.

Charles "Golden Boy" Trippi: "*Everybody's All American, all-time halfback*
who has gained more yardage in the newspapers than on the field."

Hugh "Bones" Taylor, Washington Redskins: "*Caught 25 passes,*
511 yards and 6 touchdowns
though plagued by mysterious fever throughout his rookie year."

The Late Flight

Des Moines man arrives dead at airport.
Authorities investigate if he died mid-flight
or before boarding.

–Newspaper headline

Whenever someone spoke he kept silent;
when everyone was silent he kept still.
Security had waved its wand between his legs.
Why live, only to land . . . there?

In Des Moines, the older part of town, the houses
crowd so you can hear the neighbors breathe.
All that prairie gone to soy,
to box stores and vinyl siding.

For those who need a little extra time in boarding . . . :
He hadn't, I noticed, didn't touch
his beef and garden medley—overcooked—
nor a cocktail for four dollars, beer and wine for three.

"We're very satisfied
the passenger was alive
when he boarded our aircraft,"
the company's statement read.

Missed connection? Had he waited on standby
just too long? No bird
saw him struggle with his wings
and fold them up mid stroke.

Away

This is grandma's hair which she cut off in the 20's when short hair became popular. Before that, she wore it penned up in a "pug." It is "virgin" hair (never permed) which makes it more valuable (wig makers may buy it) so check before discarding (I never wanted to sell it because it was my mom's and she had such beautiful hair!)

–Note found in a box

Unfolded from clear plastic wrapping,
the two horsetails lay on the desk in lamplight.
Almost three feet from the twine-bound end to wisps,
colors play, different as shades of afternoon
gone brown and blonde. Waves curve, cushion soft
when bunched, each lock fine.
The hair smells of powder, faint
but not old, not old at all.
How lucky that eighty
years ago styles changed so
drastically, all at once. That a woman over forty
still cared about that. Never to be sold
but perhaps traded for all the years in between,
exchanged for one moment: the pearl-handled scissors
her stepmother brought from Denmark, two slow, angled cuts,
straight, deliberate,
yet unmasculine, defining. Where to save it? For
what use? Where to put it away?

In My Mother's Drawer

Lint roller   Packer decal   a bag of tops for lost pens.

Two opened rolls of peppermint BreathSavers,
"Works even after the mint is gone."

4-in-1 screwdriver/bottle opener
for donors to the VFW
("Good luck," says the many-leaved clover on its face.)

Hand mirror from a long-merged building and loan.

Menthelatum stick *best if used before . . . .*   Everything
is half gone, still good, thought worth saving.

Like the newspaper
clippings: Ghandi's Seven Sins,

Dear Abby
from a May 31st ("*Work as if
your life were in peril.
It really is.*"),

Cousin Ralph's obituary, time of visitation underlined in black.

And typed out on a scrap cut to fit these words:
1 box golden raisins
Gin—pour over to cover
Let stand (about one week) until liquor
disappears.
EAT ONLY 9 RAISINS A DAY.
Results in less than a month.

Motion. Pictures.

Over a scotch, which I don't usually drink, I can remember old snapshots without looking: my wife with arms spread, body lilting, in dark glasses, flower-patterned silk slacks riffling in the breeze. I took the picture from inside the *roulette*, the little house trailer they rented us in a small town in Quebec because their motel was full.

Another scotch brings my brother by a campfire years before, night shot, snow on the ground at the continental divide, and a carved wooden head we found while scrounging for kindling, and then told weird stories about through the evening. The next morning the car wouldn't start.

I feel superior to the younger versions of myself pictured: looking overmatched by a stuffed backpack, feigned ease with an awkward series of girlfriends, uncomfortable even on the dustcover of an early book, as if trying to see in the window across the street.

With decades of practice, living is mostly easier, a stroll through the park towards the center of town, leaves ankle deep, past the statue of the great general, marked by pigeons. To know the way home you need to have been gone enough times. To prosper you might need to take up something new you'll never be good at, like the oboe or Persian cooking. But no need to foment crisis—as if middle age were truly the middle and not a euphemism for a long last act that leaves an imaginary audience peeking at their wristwatches. They've got reservations at a wine bar after the show.

Buddies

Three of us are paddling kayaks on a lazy river, a hot day.
We like it that you leave a car at put in, another at take out,
can't turn back along the way. Middle age
is like the place on the river where we are right now,
a slow bend, carp sunning in the shallows, mud
baking on shore. Our brains so many eggs, the sun
on dirty water, brown from the runoff of towns upstream.

Larry is snapping hopeless pictures of a heron
fishing motionless in the shallows, a tiny dot on his LCD.
Suddenly that bird gives up, flies low
directly overhead, as if smiling for Larry's camera.
"There you go, man," Chaz says, "there you go!" And soon

we're talking about luck like this, moments of apparent grace,
and using phrases we can use to agree with anything:
There you go, man, there you go!

"I can't paddle next weekend, too busy with the dating service!"
There you go, man, there you go!
"Since my layoff at the plant, I'm a lot less depressed about work."
There you go, man, there you go!

To be this agreeable is to fish in easy waters
and fly from point to point hardly lifting a wing,
guided by instincts so true they seem to be smiling.
It's merely our turn on the planet.
We paddle slowly and the brown river moves.

Larry is divorced and going out again;
Chaz and I are not, and not. Advice from the two of us
is best left in the distant cave of the 1970s.

"I don't think I should wait around and let my ex just . . . "
Why would ya?

"I should shop around before I commit to a woman who . . . "
Why wouldn't ya?
"My little brother thinks I should date that girl
in my welding class at the technical school."
There you go, man, there you go!

"Fuck buddies," Chaz intones.

His son tells him kids say now they're fuck buddies.
Just a weekly romp, then back to the daily wars.
The concept is strange to us, in no cave, no
old vault we have the combination for,
and not in the silver maples along the shoreline,
turning their light leaves in wind, almost against the rules.

Maybe *that's* what you need, one of us says,
and after the silence after the laughter,
a pair of eagles lifts off from a pair of trees
and every sunning carp knows to flip into the brown river and hide.

III

Why God Permits Bad Art

I'm in a hotel lobby packed with balloons,
in my hobnail boots, hoping to check in
without stomping on some little kid's birthday.
The inflated colors look pretty good arranged this way.

I know that God hasn't goofed too often,
and if everybody leaned one way in the cosmos
like wet clothes on a line, the flop of shirt *and* sheet,
then we couldn't tell truth from style.

This is after all the God who gave us love
—but who also brought us infatuation,
marking, perhaps, an off day for the Big Guy
with the drives arcing beyond the green on the cosmos' long par five.

A drummer I know says no independence
without coordination, no sizzle
without the sock—*And there you has jazz.*
Let's say he's right. What's more, love

was no mulligan, birthdays
don't come every week,
and my silence doesn't mean I don't approve
of anything anyone else has made.

Revising Myself

The dénouement of closing time:
The young looking to die in each other's arms for one night only,
the muscled bouncers wanting simply to go home,
traffic thinning, cops idling on the corner.

We only regret what we *didn't* do,
a fellow drinker tells me, a way of urging us on, who are too old for this.

But the next morning, sun on my face, facing south these winter afternoons,
I want only to check the TV listings, chuck most ambition
to the compost pile with the coffee grounds and "good ideas."
Why is that? Because I know so little, am here so long?
Because there's so much that's been done already, why try?

Because of the joke about the old men, friends so many years
they could refer to events by number and laugh: "Thirty Seven!" "Sixteen!!"
and all shed the same cloudy tear?

Action is overrated; more thought, revision always called for.
And not just to find the fat in bad lines from the past.
Not just to correct gaffs stuck like bones in a flat white throat.
No such tweak or tuck could make me the character I always wanted to be.

Jam Session, Saturday Afternoon, Mid Winter, Duluth

One regular walks to the stage like he's shat his pants,
his body a misshapen letter C, corroded
alto sax on his neckstrap. Even his cap

trembles, brim bearing
the logo of the band: "Route 66 Jazz Quartet:
where do you get your kicks?"

The notes he chooses are like trees
left in a cutover, phrases that stop
at every corner to look both ways.

Everyone in the bar is older than someone else.
The eyes of the men still follow the twenty-something
filling out a pair of jeans at the pool table.

"Here's a tune written in 1920,"
the man tells scattered applause.
"I think I got it on an old 78."

My buddy, my buddy, your buddy
misses you. He tells us
it's his birthday one more time.

Behind the bar, a wedding cake of booze bottles,
back lit. Figurines reign like bride and groom at each end,
Mae West and W.C. Fields.

On the far wall, life-sized
photos of burlesque queens, black
and white, their pasties covering what must be.

One bent at the waist
holds her breasts in her hands
as if she were serving them for dinner.

Bill Evans

Should anyone ever fail
this beautifully again,
promise me

your late conversion
won't keep you
from at least

sending word—that someone
once again
hasn't wasted life

on certainty.
Heroin, counterpoint,
Ravel, cocaine:

When he got into something
he really got into it.
It seems too much

to deny a man
slumped forehead to the keys
and their impossible jagged line

like black and white starlight,
his right arm limp with dead nerves,
while the left hand turns out the stars.

The shirt someone buttoned for him,
cigarettes on spring days,
the background chatter that wasn't there. Isn't.

How long it takes to die this way
when it rains outside, and within.
I suppose when the wind behaves,

the waves take note.
I'll hear that someone
came through the revolving door

again into
the shapeless dark
and began to play.

The Lesson

The horns I used to play in weekend bands
asleep in their closet cases,
my wife has started piano lessons
and practices daily with such joy
that she gives dedication a bad name.
She's playing songs a child would play,
Skip to My Lou, the Bridge of Avignon.
She works her Alberti bass in her left hand,
hits the same wrong note more than once,
and I look up from the dishes in the sink
or the news on TV and bark *NO!*
She's never angry, never replies. Just runs
the phrase again, right this time. Over time
she's improving, little by little, maybe a little
every day.

Conversations with Su Tung P'o

East Wind stirs fine dust on the roads.
Old moments snow down from north of here.

Old poet, new friend, are you lost out of time, out of place?
Are the leaves of your book in disarray like loose petals

blurred like phrases in our uncommon language?
Or are those the pages of the calendar torn

and recollected again in random order?
Are you here with me in the cloudshine and windfire

or buried in your book
a milenium past?

*

Slack Season—just right for roadside drinking.
We have more in common than I thought!

Let's get drunk and recite each other's lines out of order.
Let's break the law and convene

the new congress of lyric we'll establish,
far from God and the Emperor.

Lay that book aside and lie next to the fire
for we can always write new books

because we want to, not because the Palace says we must,
not because the muses say we can. Let's be somebody else

this slack season, just right for failing memory,
just right for the comfortable ditch.

*

Life passes quickly, hedged by sorrow.
It's all gravity collected in a jar like old water

It's all just peelings in the sink.
In a little while the moon rises in front of the eastern hills.

I grieve less for home than the years that are lost,
trouble deep as dust there, and no good mop, no good map.

And so each year I hate to see autumn go.
You'd think all that practice would make it easier.

But beauty must select and scrutinize. Can there be
but one cello in the empty warehouse,

one *erhu* in the governor's bower,
any weather not significant to someone?

*

Maybe we can sleep back to back on the warm floor,
like a couple of Sung gentlemen, a couple

of Americans camping in the same tent.
This death business could turn out to be serious.

File it under Needs Immediate Attention.
File it under The Plum Blossoms Falling Not Far From the Lake.

Who says a poem should be about one subject?
For instance, I have no way of knowing what you knew.

Friend poet, I will pass on the lines of yours I don't need.
I'm bound to forget them anyway as they come true.

*

It's alleged I lack courage of conviction.
I look in the window glass to see if my smile is on straight.

I *have stood a long time in twilight mist,*
failing as the ordinary must fail, straining to be seen in the dark.

Is there no direction to look
not flirting with success?

Like a hat gone out of style, I know, I know.
It gets worse the older I grow.

*

I could buy and sell like any vendor I see
wrapped in coal smoke on the street.

That which isn't Art? I too dislike it, so talk all you want.
Funny, I never could keep my mouth shut.

You could wish me a second chance, but you won't.
You know I was young for too long.

A year ago today the rain fell,
I still remember.

Practice

Paul Wellstone

The mayor, local clergy, president of the U—they took turns introducing each other
and the Dalai Lama, who needed no introduction.

It was bright summer on the street outside, an odd-
numbered year. I thought the campaign hadn't started yet.

Then came that choppy-armed gesture opponents put on tape loops in attack ads,
the slight stoop and limp of MS, the apparent

desire to levitate. He spoke as if there were a fire in the aisles,
and only he could see it. As if to move the boulder of discourse straight uphill.

As if life in the moment need not mean just buying something.
As if there were a passion that must be ours.

*

Far from the site of his disappearance, traffic goes on, a path of lights
along I-94 into Wisconsin. Friday night in town, no one can get a table.

In the exurbs, housewives load weekend groceries
through the tailgates of giant cars. The crowded parking lots, even in

the freezing rain, run off to the abandoned field
next to be developed. In the cities, the children of the poor

will still rise tomorrow.
The day is dark and cold.

*

A small man hunched at the podium, beloved by many, revered by his own
—he's not running for anything. His saffron and scarlet robes are rivers

draped over the shoulderless body. Question: *Don't you hate the Chinese for what they did to your country?* His Holiness: *Sometimes.*

His Holiness: *If you find what I say useful,*
then I hope you will try to practice it.

Dick's Left Wing Bait Shop

If you want to own the means of production take a jig and pig
down to Every Man Lake when the wind's coming out of the south

in opposition to the oppression of the ruling class
or act locally and drop a vibrating crankbait

into the streets when the masses are just starting to feed
right after sunset late in the season

when bread rations have been slashed and stove wood is harder to find
than a quiet stretch of stream bank.

A freeze dried minnow on a Lindy Rig is as good
as power from the barrel of a gun

and when I saw his stringer full of heavy largemouths
I started agitating in my tacklebox

and Leon said what are you looking for
and I answered comrade I'm using what you're using

Leon said now *that's* Party discipline
I said Leon there's no class nature only bass nature and this one

had a huge fat belly like he swallowed a landlord whole
and I'm not going to even guess how much that lunker weighed.

I'll just let you know I didn't get him into the boat
not alone anyway.

House in the Suburbs

Those coffee machines still exist—I saw one at an Interstate wayside in Iowa—the ones where the paper cup drops and dark brew follows, then liquid white, then clear to taste. I want to say marriage is like that machine. Like that hot water transfigured to coffee, pouring from on high. Or marriage is like the coffee's charge that keeps you awake behind the wheel. But it's really more like a house in the suburbs—location its single virtue, its chief disadvantage. There's sufficient quiet, but no ethnic restaurants or arty films. It's easy to get lost when everything looks the same.

*

At rush hour, a day last winter, I forgot to tell you about the three deer, one young, I saw motionless (the way only deer can be), eating grass at the intersection of Boone and 42nd, the field that belongs to the Catholic cemetery. And this morning, while you slept in and I was watering, the pair of robins with the nest on the post top beneath the summer porch dive bombed me from two angles in turns. I call them Mr. and Mrs. Rickenbacker, am encouraged by their relationship, but today fended them off with the hose. I worry they'll hurt themselves and leave no bird to raise the fluffball still cold and hungry in the nest.

*

If I write something addressed to you when it's really for anyone to read, that's because I want readers to feel connected to me. To feel they've been connected for a long time, and to carry the illusion that I can be trusted, or need to be.

Moon Repair

Slate skies in that time of November
you used to like, used to like
writing about, the prevailing wind no wind at all
by day's end, like a sentence you looked forward to writing
and thus never would.

*

The old Comiskey Park,
Southside darkness
even like rich milk
over the dome of light
and the vendor's cry
"Men: Beer! Beer!"
that seemed to mean something.
I was too young to say just what.

The Sox were losing, couldn't hit,
the Yanks between dynasties,
Maris traded, late Mantle gimped
in the visitor's dugout.

*

The joke about the restaurant on the moon:
Good food, but no atmosphere.

Remember that Auden was unimpressed
that men had walked there,

thought of the junk they left behind
whenever he looked up.

*

Some people say the glass is half empty, some half full.

Some say, *What glass?*
I don't see a glass.

Some people I guess
aren't looking for ways
to think about the rest of their lives.
Like those phonies who told me as a boy
"Just be yourself." How I hated that advice,
which clearly wasn't working for them.

It was as if the music had stopped
and no one had a chair.

Some people say, *What moon?*
I can't see a moon.

*

A future you don't need to drive,
the past you'd still like to live,
that trolley across from the fire station, tracks torn up,
that little TV store
where they sold little TVs
—ok, not that,
but the corner store on the block your grandparents lived,
once a grocery, now "Look Over New Portable Models for 1961!"

Grandpa's white frame house once a small barn, the story went.
The lawn you mowed when they were too old to.

*

Those guys who read the Bible making circles around it,

those guys who almost didn't make it back.
The guy who smuggled the bowling ball into space
and rolled a perfect game in tranquility.
The guy who smuggled dope and rolled that.

Imagine the craters failing,
the speed of light still young.

Road sign in space: "SLOW: MOON REPAIR."
Such dysfunction, blue spot on a dark map.

*

Something to do with mountains
and what won't grow in the shade.

Something to do with mending,
with waking in church.

If you don't know where you're going
you'll never know when you've gone too far.

*

Early Man drove to the edge of town in his Chrysler,
civil twilight giving way to patterns of stars
sailors far away might read for meaning.
They believed gravity collected in a glass like seawater,

planets on their long leash enjoying shore leave
—ok, I made that one up, too, and much
of what you'll find here. Blame it on the times,
that we want not truth, but night.

Then the moon rises like a bag left unattended at the airport,
—so much fuss about danger, and it's only stuffed with light.

Marriage

I awaken on edge from the dream: my wife
had set up rickety shelves in the hall
—teetering eyesores, sliver repositories.
She'd filled each unlevel space with thrift store
knick knacks, junk on sale, piles
of papers, not mine, not to be touched or read.
The guest room lay fallow, her last week's wardrobe

in cotton islands on the floor,
the dining room table place set with the *Daily Record*,
a year's worth, and not this year's, some clippings
about her sons and pithy comic strips
set apart and guarded by a hand-
lettered construction paper sign: KEEP! DO NOT TOSS!!
In the kitchen each cupboard was open, each drawer ajar,
and every dish we own draining in the sink.

I do not speak of it now, with her
still four-a.m.-asleep beside me.
I'm bent upright like a flexed joint, jolted awake,
just this moment putting into place
what has really happened and what has not,
the room too hot, the door blown shut,
the house locked tight and everyone safe in their dark.

Wall Painting in Chicago Bar: "Richard J. Daley, Mayor"

It's three blocks from where my Cantonese in-laws live since they moved out of Chinatown. Bridgeport, so-called: no bridge, no port, but working class. I'd thought the neighborhood tough—afraid to go out, lock your door at night. But one couple on the corner stools, who could be Torres or Rodriguez, toasts me with pints of MGD, while guys with broad faces of Poles wear White Sox caps and watch Notre Dame football on the one working TV. A mixed race couple plays chess near the back exit, its locked door and sign that reads: M*ust Remain Open During Business Hours.*

When my stepsons, young men now, invited me to go shoot pool, I said, "What?" thinking I'd misunderstood. Thanksgiving night, snow in the air but not on the ground, all three of us refugees from cousins, uncles, and Mom (aka, my wife), we're visiting from out of town, shooting against a couple guys named Vito and Ceasar who belong to this parish, orderlies at the hospital we walked past to get to the bar. Crucifixes dangle from their necks as they eye the corner pocket.

Notre Dame goes ahead by a touchdown ("They'll lose," Vito says, not looking up from his shot).

Leftover turkey cools throughout the neighborhood, and we're warming up in the neon beer sign light. The balls rattle alive when Vito breaks, explode like neutrons, but nothing drops. The older patrons have these days off work. Some argue about bowl picks and the Bears; the young buzz on cell phones, like my sons: *Are you there? Are you in Texas? No, dude, I'm in Chicago, shooting pool and doing shots.*

Richard J. Daley's beneficent gaze softens the cone of light above the pool table, Mayor Daley the first, in his black suit and red tie. The white below the iris in each eye gives him a hound-like steadfastness. He's dogged for the contentment of his ward. Like Mary (aka the Virgin Mother) he looks skyward for bliss, and perhaps for votes, keeping watch over the neighborhood, over Vito, Cesar, the bartender, and us, as Southern Cal threatens to score.

"Completed in '53, retouched 2000," the inscription below the portrait reads. The year I was born and the year I realized I was as happy as I'm likely to get, unretouched and unrevisited. For this is Bridgeport, no bridge in sight, no port of call for any ship. We're on the green felt sea, on the exit ramp of life, we older patrons, the evening of this holiday my in-laws don't celebrate—rice, curried lamb, and bean curd sheets for our turkey day repast. But I'm not Cantonese, not ethnic working class, not Hispanic and sitting at the corner stool. There are a lot of things I'm not, here without my wife (aka, all that I have in this flat world), with my grown sons and the good shots they leave the other guys.

Notre Dame scores again as time runs out. I'm going to bank the six off the rail and set up the eight in the side.

Acknowledgments

Thanks to readers whose advice proved so helpful: Gwen Hart, Casey Lord, Jean Prokott, Patti See, and my graduate poetry students at Minnesota State, Mankato.

Special thanks to those who helped shape the manuscript: Bruce Taylor, Mark Halperin, Keith Ratzlaff, Christina Olson, and editor extrordinaire Jenny Fandel.

Thanks to Richard Mathews, Sean Donnelly, and everyone at UT Press.

Grants from Minnesota State University, Mankato, including the Distinguished Faculty Scholar Award, supported the creation and assemblage of these poems.

Thanks to the following journals in which some of these poems originally appeared, often in a different version and sometimes under a different title:

Black Clock: "Found Poems."
Blue Earth Review: "Lines Abandoned by My Students" and "November 22."
Blue Road Reader: "What to Write," "Where It Stays," "*O dwóch takich, co ukradli księżyc*," and "Eastern Poland, 2003."
Brevity: "House in the Suburbs."
Connecticut Review: "What to Want."
Epicenters: "Dick's Left Wing Bait Shop" and "Why God Permits Bad Art."
Great River Review: "The Past."
Green Mountains Review: "Last Places."
Iowa Review: "I Kept the Part About Turning Fifty."
Iron Horse Literary Review: "Religion."
New Letters: "In My Mother's Drawer," "The Late Flight," and "Credit."
Nimrod: "Buddies."
Poetry Daily: "In My Mother's Drawer."
Tampa Review: "Ideas of Order"
Waterstone Review: "American" and "How to Live."

Pages 64-66: In "Conversations with Su Tung P'o"—italicized lines are from *Selected Poems of Su Tung-p'o*, translated by Burton Watson (Copper Canyon Press, 1994).

About the Author

Richard Terrill is the author of a previous collection of poems, *Coming Late to Rachmaninoff*, winner of the Minnesota Book Award, as well as two books of creative nonfiction, *Fakebook: Improvisations on a Journey Back to Jazz* and *Saturday Night in Baoding: A China Memoir*, winner of the Associated Writing Programs Award for nonfiction. He has been awarded fellowships from the National Endowment for the Arts, the Wisconsin and Minnesota State Arts Boards, the Jerome Foundation, the MacDowell Colony, and the Bread Loaf Writers' Conference. His essays and poems have appeared widely in journals such as *North American Review*, *Tampa Review*, *Iowa Review*, *Fourth Genre*, *River Teeth*, and *New Letters*. He has taught as a Fulbright professor in China, Korea, and Poland, and currently teaches writing in the MFA program at Minnesota State University, Mankato, where he is a Distinguished Faculty Scholar. He works as a jazz saxophone player with the Larry McDonough Quartet. He lives in Minneapolis.

About the Book

Almost Dark has been composed in Garamond Premier Pro types based on the roman fonts created in Paris by Claude Garamond (c. 1480-1561) and the complementary italics of Robert Granjon (1513-1589). The original sixteenth century typefaces were adapted for digital composition by Robert Slimbach of Adobe Fonts. The cover and dust jacket featuring a photograph taken in Kraków, Poland, by Jurek Durczak were designed by Ana Montalvo and Richard Mathews, with titling in ITC Goudy Sans and Tiepolo. The book was designed and composed by Richard Mathews at the University of Tampa Press.

Poetry from the University of Tampa Press

Jenny Browne, *At Once*

Jenny Browne, *The Second Reason*

Christopher Buckley, *Rolling the Bones**

Richard Chess, *Chair in the Desert*

Richard Chess, *Tekiah*

Richard Chess, *Third Temple*

Kevin Jeffery Clarke, *The Movie of Us*

Jane Ellen Glasser, *Light Persists**

Benjamin S. Grossberg, *Sweet Core Orchard**

Kathleen Jesme, *Fire Eater*

Steve Kowit, *The First Noble Truth**

Lance Larsen, *In All Their Animal Brilliance**

Julia B. Levine, *Ask**

Julia B. Levine, *Ditch-tender*

Sarah Maclay, *Whore**

Sarah Maclay, *The White Bride*

John Willis Menard, *Lays in Summer Lands*

Kent Shaw, *Calenture**

Barry Silesky, *This Disease*

Jordan Smith, *For Appearances**

Jordan Smith, *The Names of Things Are Leaving*

Lisa M. Steinman, *Carslaw's Sequences*

Marjorie Stelmach, *Bent upon Light*

Marjorie Stelmach, *A History of Disappearance*

Richard Terrill, *Coming Late to Rachmaninoff*

Richard Terrill, *Almost Dark*

Matt Yurdana, *Public Gestures*

* Denotes winner of the Tampa Review Prize for Poetry